BARACK OBAMA
ON
CIVIL RIGHTS

The Most Important Speeches on Civil Rights

from Our 44th President

Words and speeches of
Barack Obama

Compiled by Sheila Jackson

Infotainment Press

Arrangement © 2011 Infotainment Press.
Speeches by Barack Obama while serving as President of the United States.
Compiled and edited by Sheila Jackson

This book contains fourteen of the most important set of speeches from President Barack Obama on the topic of Civil Rights. Chapters include President's reflections on Martin Luther King, Jr, the thoughts he shared during the funeral for Dr. Dorothy Height, as well as the comments he made at the repeal of Don't Ask Don't Tell. This rare collection offers powerful insight into the man and character of President Obama.

Printed in the United States of America.

Table of Contents

Chapter 1

Remarks by the President Upon Signing the Lilly Ledbetter Bill

January 29, 2009

All right. Everybody please have a seat. Well, this is a wonderful day. (Applause.) First of all, it is fitting that the very first bill that I sign — the Lilly Ledbetter Fair Pay Restoration Act — (applause) — that it is upholding one of this nation's founding principles: that we are all created equal, and each deserve a chance to pursue our own version of happiness.

It's also fitting that we're joined today by the woman after whom this bill is named — someone who Michelle and I have had the privilege to get to know ourselves. And it is fitting that we are joined this morning by the first woman Speaker of the House of Representatives, Nancy Pelosi. (Applause.) It's appropriate that this is the first bill we do together. We could not have done it without her. Madam Speaker, thank you for your extraordinary work. And to all the sponsors and members of Congress and leadership who helped to make this day possible.

Lilly Ledbetter did not set out to be a trailblazer or a household name. She was just a good hard worker who did her job — and she did it well — for nearly two decades before discovering that for years, she was paid less than her male colleagues for doing the very same work. Over the course of her career, she lost more than $200,000 in salary, and even more in pension and Social Security benefits — losses that she still feels today.

Now, Lilly could have accepted her lot and moved on. She could have decided that it wasn't worth the hassle and the harassment that would inevitably come with speaking up for what she deserved. But instead, she decided that there was a principle at stake, something worth fighting for. So she set out on a journey that would take more than ten years, take her all the way to the Supreme Court of the United States, and lead to this day and this bill which will help others get the justice that she was denied.

Because while this bill bears her name, Lilly knows that this story isn't just about her. It's the story of women across this country still earning just 78 cents for every dollar men earn — women of color even less — which means that today, in the year 2009, countless women are still losing thousands of dollars in salary, income and retirement savings over the course of a lifetime.

Equal pay is by no means just a women's issue — it's a family issue. It's about parents who find themselves with less money for tuition and child care; couples who wind up with less to retire on; households where one breadwinner is paid less than she deserves; that's the difference between affording the mortgage — or not; between keeping the heat on, or paying the doctor bills — or not. And in this economy, when so many folks are already working harder for less and struggling to get by, the last thing they can afford is losing part of each month's paycheck to simple and plain discrimination.

So signing this bill today is to send a clear message: that making our economy work means making sure it works for everybody; that there are no second-class citizens in our workplaces; and that it's not just unfair and illegal, it's bad for business to pay somebody less because of their gender or their age or their race or their ethnicity, religion or disability; and that justice isn't about some abstract legal theory, or footnote in a casebook. It's about how our laws affect the daily lives and the daily realities of people: their ability to make a living and care for their families and achieve their goals.

Ultimately, equal pay isn't just an economic issue for millions of Americans and their families, it's a question of who we are — and whether we're truly living up to our fundamental ideals; whether we'll do our part, as generations before us, to ensure those words put on paper some 200 years ago really mean something — to breathe new life into them with a more enlightened understanding that is appropriate for our time.

That is what Lilly Ledbetter challenged us to do. And today, I sign this bill not just in her honor, but in the honor of those who came before — women like my grandmother, who worked in a bank all her life, and even after she hit that glass ceiling, kept getting up and giving her best every day, without complaint, because she wanted something better for me and my sister.

And I sign this bill for my daughters, and all those who will come after us, because I want them to grow up in a nation that values their contributions, where there are no limits to their dreams and they have opportunities their mothers and grandmothers never could have imagined.

In the end, that's why Lilly stayed the course. She knew it was too late for her — that this bill wouldn't undo the years of injustice she faced or restore the earnings she was denied. But this grandmother from Alabama kept on fighting, because she was thinking about the next generation. It's what we've always done in America — set our sights high for ourselves, but even higher for our children and our grandchildren.

And now it's up to us to continue this work. This bill is an important step — a simple fix to ensure fundamental fairness for American workers — and I want to thank this remarkable and bipartisan group of legislators who worked so hard to get it passed. And I want to thank all the advocates who are in the audience who worked so hard to get it passed. This is only the beginning. I know that if we stay focused, as Lilly did — and keep standing for what's right, as Lilly did — we will close that pay gap and we will make sure that our daughters have the same rights, the same chances, and the same freedoms to pursue their dreams as our sons.

So thank you, Lilly Ledbetter. (Applause.)

Chapter 2

Remarks By The President At The 102nd Abraham Lincoln Association Annual Banquet

February 12, 2009

It is wonderful to be back in Springfield, the city where I got my start in elected office, where I served for nearly a decade, and where I launched my candidacy for President two years ago, this week – on the steps of the Old State Capitol where Abraham Lincoln served and prepared for the presidency.

It was here, nearly one hundred and fifty years ago, that the man whose life we are celebrating today bid farewell to this city he had come to call his own. On a platform at a train station not far from where we're gathered, Lincoln turned to the crowd that had come to see him off, and said, "To this place, and the kindness of these people, I owe everything." Being here tonight, surrounded by all of you, I share his sentiments.

But looking out at this room, full of so many who did so much for me, I'm also reminded of what Lincoln once said to a favor-seeker who claimed it was his efforts that made the difference in the election. Lincoln asked him, "So you think you made me President?" "Yes," the man replied, "under Providence, I think I did." "Well," said Lincoln, "it's a pretty mess you've got me into. But I forgive you."

It is a humbling task, marking the bicentennial of our 16th President's birth – humbling for me in particular, I think, for the presidency of this singular figure in so many ways made my own story possible.

Here in Springfield, it is easier, perhaps, to reflect on Lincoln the man rather than the marble giant, before Gettysburg and Antietam, Fredericksburg and Bull Run, before emancipation was proclaimed and the captives were set free. In 1854, Lincoln was simply a Springfield lawyer, who'd served just a single term in Congress. Possibly in his law office, his feet on a cluttered desk, his sons playing around him, his clothes a bit too small to fit his uncommon frame, he put some thoughts on paper for what purpose we do not know:

"The legitimate object of government," he wrote, "is to do for the people what needs to be done, but which they can not, by individual effort, do at all, or do so well, by themselves."

To do for the people what needs to be done but which they cannot do on their own. It is a simple statement. But it answers a central question of Abraham Lincoln's life. Why did he land on the side of union? What was it that made him so unrelenting in pursuit of victory that he was willing to test the Constitution he ultimately preserved? What was it that led this man to give his last full measure of devotion so that our nation might endure? These are not easy questions to answer, and I cannot know if I am right. But I suspect that his devotion to union came not from a belief that government always had the answer. It came not from a failure to understand our individual rights and responsibilities. This rugged rail-splitter, born in a log cabin of pioneer stock; who cleared a path through the woods as a boy; who lost a mother and a sister to the rigors of frontier life; who taught himself all he knew – this man, our first Republican President, knew, better than anyone, what it meant to pull yourself up by your bootstraps. He understood that strain of personal liberty and self-reliance at the heart of the American experience.

But he also understood something else. He recognized that while each of us must do our part, work as hard as we can, and be as responsible as we can – in the end, there are certain things we cannot do on our own. There are certain things we can only do together. There are certain things only a union can do.

Only a union could harness the courage of our pioneers to settle the American west, which is why he passed a Homestead Act giving a tract of land to anyone seeking a stake in our growing economy.

Only a union could foster the ingenuity of our farmers, which is why he set up land-grant colleges that taught them how to make the most of their land while giving their children an education that let them dream the American dream.

Only a union could speed our expansion and connect our coasts with a transcontinental railroad, and so, even in the midst of civil war, he built one. He fueled new enterprises with a national currency, spurred innovation, and ignited America's imagination with a national academy of sciences, believing we must, as he put it, add "the fuel of interest to the fire of genius in the discovery...of new and useful things." And on this day, that is also the bicentennial of Charles Darwin's birth, let us renew that commitment to science and innovation once more

Only a union could serve the hopes of every citizen – to knock down the barriers to opportunity and give each and every person the chance to pursue the American dream. Lincoln understood what Washington understood when he led farmers, craftsmen, and shopkeepers to rise up against an empire. What Roosevelt understood when he lifted us from Depression, built an arsenal of democracy, and created the largest middle-class in history with the GI Bill. It's what Kennedy understood when he sent us to the moon.

All these presidents recognized that America is – and always has been – more than a band of thirteen colonies, more than a bunch of Yankees and Confederates, more than a collection of Red States and Blue States. We are the United States of America and there isn't any dream beyond our reach, any obstacle that can stand in our way, when we recognize that our individual liberty is served, not negated, by a recognition of the common good.

That is the spirit we are called to show once more. The challenges we face are very different now. Two wars, and an economic crisis unlike any we have seen in our lifetime. Jobs have been lost. Pensions are gone. Families' dreams have been endangered. Health care costs are exploding. Schools are falling short. And we have an energy crisis that is hampering our economy, threatening our planet, and enriching our adversaries.

And yet, while our challenges may be new, they did not come about overnight. Ultimately, they result from a failure to meet the test that Lincoln set. To be sure, there have been times in our history when our government has misjudged what we can do by individual effort alone, and what we can only do together; when it has done things that people can – or should – do for themselves. Our welfare system, for example, too often dampened individual initiative, discouraging people from taking responsibility for their own upward mobility. With respect to education, we have all too frequently lost sight of the role of parents, rather than government, in cultivating a thirst for knowledge and instilling those qualities of a good character – hard work, discipline, and integrity – that are so important to educational achievement and professional success.

But in recent years, we've seen the pendulum swing too far in the opposite direction. It's a philosophy that says every problem can be solved if only government would step out of the way; that if government were just dismantled, divvied up into tax breaks, and handed out to the wealthiest among us, it would somehow benefit us all. Such knee-jerk disdain for government – this constant rejection of any common endeavor – cannot rebuild our levees or our roads or our bridges. It cannot refurbish our schools or modernize our health care system; lead to the next medical discovery or yield the research and technology that will spark a clean energy economy.

Only a nation can do these things. Only by coming together, all of us, and expressing that sense of shared sacrifice and responsibility – for ourselves and one another – can we do the work that must be done in this country. That is the very definition of being American.

It is only by rebuilding our economy and fostering the conditions of growth that willing workers can find a job, companies can find capital, and the entrepreneurial spirit that is the key to our competitiveness can flourish. It is only by unleashing the potential of alternative fuels that we will lower our energy bills and raise our industries' sights, make our nation safer and our planet cleaner. It is only by remaking our schools for the 21st century that our children will get those good jobs so they can make of their lives what they will. It is only by coming together to do what people need done that we will, in Lincoln's words, "lift artificial weights from all shoulders [and give] all an unfettered start, and a fair chance, in the race of life."

That is what is required of us – now and in the years ahead. We will be remembered for what we choose to make of this moment. And when posterity looks back on our time, as we are looking back on Lincoln's, I do not want it said that we saw an economic crisis, but did not stem it. That we saw our schools decline and our bridges crumble, but did not rebuild them. That the world changed in the 21st century, but America did not lead it. That we were consumed with small things when we were called to do great things. Instead, let them say that this generation – our generation – of Americans rose to the moment and gave America a new birth of freedom and opportunity in our time.

These are trying days and they will grow tougher in the months to come. There will be moments when our doubts rise and our hopes recede. But let's always remember that we, as a people, have been here before. There were times when our revolution itself seemed altogether improbable, when the union was all but lost, and fascism seemed set to prevail. And yet, what earlier generations discovered – what we must rediscover right now – is that it is precisely when we are in the deepest valley, precisely when the climb is steepest, that Americans relearn how to take the mountaintop. Together. As one nation. As one people. That is how we will beat back our present dangers. That is how we will surpass what trials may come. And that is how we will do what Lincoln called on us to do, and "nobly save...the last best hope of earth." Thank you, God Bless you, and may God Bless America.

Chapter 3

Remarks by the President at the Dedication of Abraham Lincoln Hall

March 12, 2009

Thank you, General Wilson, for the wonderful introduction and your hospitality. Thank you to Secretary Gates and Admiral Mullen for the extraordinary service that they render to this country. I want to acknowledge the other members of the Joint Chiefs of Staff who are doing outstanding work and have been a great support to me and Ambassador Ross.

To each of you who are here, for your service to our country and your commitment to our security, I want to say thank you on behalf of the American people. You know, I think so highly of NDU that I picked one of your alumni, General Jim Jones, to be my National Security Advisor. (Applause.)

I know many of you have served in harm's way, and for that you have the respect of a grateful nation. And before I go any further, I want to acknowledge all of our troops now serving overseas. They have shouldered an awesome — (applause) — they have shouldered an awesome responsibility. They have performed brilliantly. And they have the full support of the American people.

Today, it is my privilege to join you in dedicating this building to the memory of President Abraham Lincoln. We know, of course, that there are many monuments to Lincoln's memory across this country.

His words are written into stately walls, and his image is printed on our currency. His story is taught in our schools, and his name is synonymous with freedom. You and I live in the union that he saved, and we inherited the progress that he made possible.

Yet despite this far-reaching legacy, it is still — to quote the man himself — "altogether fitting and proper" that we should set aside this ground, and dedicate this hall, in his memory — because Lincoln's presidency was characterized by war, even as his ambition was a just and lasting peace. Here, in this indispensable institution, we find a living legacy to that ambition. Here, at National Defense University, men and women come together to think, to learn, and to seek new strategies to defend our union, while pursuing the goal of a just and lasting peace.

The grounds that make up this campus tell us an interesting story about how America can pursue this goal. Fort McNair was built over two centuries ago to protect a young capital against invasion. Its defenses were traditional — training for soldiers, stockpiles of arms, fortifications to hold advancing armies at bay. It was overrun by a British attack in the War of 1812, and treated the wounded warriors of the Civil War in Lincoln's day.

And then, just over a century ago, President Theodore Roosevelt came here to lay the cornerstone of the Army War College. In dedicating the school, Roosevelt spoke words that resonate to this day. He said, "More and more, it has become evident in modern warfare that the efficiency of the unit, of the individual officer and the individual enlisted man is going to be the prime factor in deciding the fate of fought fields."

More than 100 years later, Roosevelt's insight remained the essential mission of this institution — the belief that even as our weapons have grown more powerful, individuals still determine the strength of our national security; the belief that individual Americans remain, as Roosevelt said, "the prime factor in deciding the fate of fought fields."

The battlefields that we now face would be unfamiliar to Lincoln and Roosevelt. The days when President Lincoln would wander down to the War Department's telegraph office to get reports from the front are long past, but the threats to our nation are real, and they are direct.

From this Fort, which was founded to defend the city of Washington against invasion, you could stand on September 11, 2001, and watch the smoke from the Pentagon billowing up across the Potomac. The attacks of 9/11 signaled the new dangers of the 21st century. And today, our people are still threatened by violent extremists, and we're still at war with terrorists in Afghanistan and Pakistan who are plotting to do us harm.

Yet terrorism and extremism make up just one part of the many challenges that confront our nation. In Iraq, we will surely face difficult days ahead as we responsibly end a war by transitioning to Iraqi control of their country. A historic economic downturn has put at stake the prosperity that underpins our strength, while putting at risk the stability of governments and the survival of people around the world. We're threatened by the spread of the world's deadliest weapons, by emerging cyber threats, and by a dependence on foreign oil that endangers our security and our planet. Poverty, disease, the persistence of conflict and genocide in the 21st century challenge our international alliances, partnerships and institutions — and must call on all of us to reexamine our assumptions.

These are the battlefields of the 21st century. These are the threats that we now face. And in these struggles, the United States of America must succeed — and we will succeed.

We also know that the old approaches won't meet the challenges of our time. Threats now move freely across borders, and the ability to do great harm lies in the hands of individuals as well as nations. No technology — no matter how smart — can stop the spread of nuclear weapons. No army — no matter how strong — can eliminate every adversary. No weapon — no matter how powerful — can erase the hatred that lies in someone's heart.

So it falls to institutions like this — and to individuals like you — to help us understand the world as it is, to develop the capacities that we need to confront emerging danger, and to act with purpose and pragmatism to turn this moment of peril into one of promise. That's how we will find new pathways to peace and security. That is the work that we must do.

Now, make no mistake: This nation will maintain our military dominance. We will have the strongest armed forces in the history of the world. And we will do whatever it takes to sustain our technological advantage, and to invest in the capabilities that we need to protect our interests, and to defeat and deter any conventional enemy.

But we also need to look beyond this conventional advantage as we develop the new approaches and new capabilities of the 21st century — and in that effort, this university must play a critical role.

Our troops are faced with complex missions. Increasingly, they're called upon to defeat nimble enemies while keeping local populations on their side. And that's why my administration is committed to growing the size of our ground forces, and to investing in the skills that can help our troops succeed in the unconventional mission that they now face. We must understand different languages and different cultures; we must study determined adversaries and developing tactics.

That's the education that takes place within the walls of this university, and that is the work that must be done to keep our nation safe. (Applause.)

America must also balance and integrate all elements of our national power. We cannot continue to push the burden on to our military alone, nor leave dormant any aspect of the full arsenal of American capability. And that's why my administration is committed to renewing diplomacy as a tool of American power, and to developing our civilian national security capabilities. This effort takes place within the walls of this university, where civilians sit alongside soldiers in the classroom. And it must continue out in the field, where American civilians can advance opportunity, enhance governance and the rule of law, and attack the causes of war around the world. We have to enlist our civilians in the same way that we enlist those members of the armed services in understanding this broad mission that we have.

Finally, we know that the United States cannot defeat global threats alone. There is no permanent American solution to the security challenges that we face within any foreign nation, nor can the world meet the tests of our time without strong American leadership. And that's why my administration is committed to comprehensive engagement with the world, including strengthened partnerships with the foreign militaries and security forces that can combat our common enemies.

Those partnerships are advanced here, within the walls of this university, where we welcome men and women from around the world to study alongside Americans, to understand our values, to forge partnerships — and hopefully friendships — that contribute to a safer world.

The lesson of history is that peace and security do not come easily. Each person who passes through this university will play a different role. Some of you will serve in uniform abroad, or help train troops here at home. Some will be diplomats, intelligence officers, or congressional staffers; others will work in the private sector. Some will rise to be senior officers and top strategists, and some of you might even decide to run for public office, although I'd warn you about that. (Laughter.)

Your story is your own, and the education that you're receiving will help you advance it. But you're here because you've also accepted the responsibility of having your story as part of the larger American story. Your story is serving your fellow citizens in the wider world. And my message to you today is simple: Your individual service makes all of the difference. You will make the decisions, large and small, that will help shape our future.

So as we dedicate this building where you and future generations will be prepared to make those choices, remember that the true strength of our nation comes not from the might of our arms or the scale of our wealth — it comes from the power of our ideals: democracy, liberty, equality, justice and unyielding hope. (Applause.)

Those ideals are embedded in our national character because generations of Americans have chosen to live them in their own lives, to advance them through their service and through their sacrifice. This is the truth that Lincoln understood — that pragmatism must serve a common purpose, a higher purpose. That's the legacy that we inherit. And that, in the end, is how government of the people, and by the people, and for the people, will endure in our time.

So thank you, God bless you, and God bless the United States of America. (Applause.)

Chapter 4

Remarks by the President at Cape Coast Castle

July 11, 2009

Michelle, the children, as well as other members of my family, just got an extraordinary tour of this castle. It is reminiscent of the trip I took to Buchenwald because it reminds us of the capacity of human beings to commit great evil. One of the most striking things that I heard was that right above the dungeons in which male captives were kept was a church, and that reminds us that sometimes we can tolerate and stand by great evil even as we think that we're doing good.

You know, I think it was particularly important for Malia and Sasha, who are growing up in such a blessed way, to be reminded that history can take very cruel turns, and hopefully one of the things that was imparted to them during this trip is their sense of obligation to fight oppression and cruelty wherever it appears, and that any group of people who are degrading another group of people have to be fought against with whatever tools we have available to us.

So obviously it's a moving experience, a moving moment. We want to thank those who arranged for the tour and the people of Ghana for preserving this history. As painful as it is, I think that it helps to teach all of us that we have to do what we can to fight against the kinds of evils that, sadly, still exist in our world, not just on this continent but in every corner of the globe.

And I think, as Americans, and as African Americans, obviously there's a special sense that on the one hand this place was a place of profound sadness; on the other hand, it is here where the journey of much of the African American experience began. And symbolically, to be able to come back with my family, with Michelle and our children, and see the portal through which the diaspora began, but also to be able to come back here in celebration with the people of Ghana of the extraordinary progress that we've made because of the courage of so many, black and white, to abolish slavery and ultimately win civil rights for all people, I think is a source of hope. It reminds us that as bad as history can be, it's also possible to overcome.

Thanks, everybody.

Chapter 5

Remarks by the President at Human Rights Campaign Dinner

October 11, 2009

Thank you so much, all of you. It is a privilege to be here tonight to open for Lady GaGa. (Applause.) I've made it. (Laughter.) I want to thank the Human Rights Campaign for inviting me to speak and for the work you do every day in pursuit of equality on behalf of the millions of people in this country who work hard in their jobs and care deeply about their families — and who are gay, lesbian, bisexual, or transgender. (Applause.)

For nearly 30 years, you've advocated on behalf of those without a voice. That's not easy. For despite the real gains that we've made, there's still laws to change and there's still hearts to open. There are still fellow citizens, perhaps neighbors, even loved ones — good and decent people — who hold fast to outworn arguments and old attitudes; who fail to see your families like their families; who would deny you the rights most Americans take for granted. And that's painful and it's heartbreaking. (Applause.) And yet you continue, leading by the force of the arguments you make, and by the power of the example that you set in your own lives — as parents and friends, as PTA members and church members, as advocates and leaders in your communities. And you're making a difference.

That's the story of the movement for fairness and equality, and not just for those who are gay, but for all those in our history who've been denied the rights and responsibilities of citizenship — (applause) — for all who've been told that the full blessings and opportunities of this country were closed to them. It's the story of progress sought by those with little influence or power; by men and women who brought about change through quiet, personal acts of compassion — and defiance — wherever and whenever they could.

It's the story of the Stonewall protests, when a group of citizens — (applause) — when a group of citizens with few options, and fewer supporters stood up against discrimination and helped to inspire a movement. It's the story of an epidemic that decimated a community — and the gay men and women who came to support one another and save one another; who continue to fight this scourge; and who have demonstrated before the world that different kinds of families can show the same compassion in a time of need. (Applause.) And it's the story of the Human Rights Campaign and the fights you've fought for nearly 30 years: helping to elect candidates who share your values; standing against those who would enshrine discrimination into our Constitution; advocating on behalf of those living with HIV/AIDS; and fighting for progress in our capital and across America. (Applause.)

This story, this fight continue now. And I'm here with a simple message: I'm here with you in that fight. (Applause.) For even as we face extraordinary challenges as a nation, we cannot — and we will not — put aside issues of basic equality. I greatly appreciate the support I've received from many in this room. I also appreciate that many of you don't believe progress has come fast enough. I want to be honest about that, because it's important to be honest among friends.

Now, I've said this before, I'll repeat it again — it's not for me to tell you to be patient, any more than it was for others to counsel patience to African Americans petitioning for equal rights half a century ago. (Applause.) But I will say this: We have made progress and we will make more. And I think it's important to remember that there is not a single issue that my administration deals with on a daily basis that does not touch on the lives of the LGBT community. (Applause.) We all have a stake in reviving this economy. We all have a stake in putting people back to work. We all have a stake in improving our schools and achieving quality, affordable health care. We all have a stake in meeting the difficult challenges we face in Iraq and Afghanistan. (Applause.)

For while some may wish to define you solely by your sexual orientation or gender identity alone, you know — and I know — that none of us wants to be defined by just one part of what makes us whole. (Applause.) You're also parents worried about your children's futures. You're spouses who fear that you or the person you love will lose a job. You're workers worried about the rising cost of health insurance. You're soldiers. You are neighbors. You are friends. And, most importantly, you are Americans who care deeply about this country and its future. (Applause.)

So I know you want me working on jobs and the economy and all the other issues that we're dealing with. But my commitment to you is unwavering even as we wrestle with these enormous problems. And while progress may be taking longer than you'd like as a result of all that we face — and that's the truth — do not doubt the direction we are heading and the destination we will reach. (Applause.)

My expectation is that when you look back on these years, you will see a time in which we put a stop to discrimination against gays and lesbians — whether in the office or on the battlefield. (Applause.) You will see a time in which we as a nation finally recognize relationships between two men or two women as just as real and admirable as relationships between a man and a woman. (Applause.) You will see a nation that's valuing and cherishing these families as we build a more perfect union — a union in which gay Americans are an important part. I am committed to these goals. And my administration will continue fighting to achieve them.

And there's no more poignant or painful reminder of how important it is that we do so than the loss experienced by Dennis and Judy Shepard, whose son Matthew was stolen in a terrible act of violence 11 years ago. In May, I met with Judy — who's here tonight with her husband — I met her in the Oval Office, and I promised her that we were going to pass an inclusive hate crimes bill — a bill named for her son. (Applause.)

This struggle has been long. Time and again we faced opposition. Time and again, the measure was defeated or delayed. But the Shepards never gave up. (Applause.) They turned tragedy into an unshakeable commitment. (Applause.) Countless activists and organizers never gave up. You held vigils, you spoke out, year after year, Congress after Congress. The House passed the bill again this week. (Applause.) And I can announce that after more than a decade, this bill is set to pass and I will sign it into law. (Applause.)

It's a testament to the decade-long struggle of Judy and Dennis, who tonight will receive a tribute named for somebody who inspired so many of us — named for Senator Ted Kennedy, who fought tirelessly for this legislation. (Applause.) And it's a testament to the Human Rights Campaign and those who organized and advocated. And it's a testament to Matthew and to others who've been the victims of attacks not just meant to break bones, but to break spirits — not meant just to inflict harm, but to instill fear. Together, we will have moved closer to that day when no one has to be afraid to be gay in America. (Applause.) When no one has to fear walking down the street holding the hand of the person they love. (Applause.)

But we know there's far more work to do. We're pushing hard to pass an inclusive employee non-discrimination bill. (Applause.) For the first time ever, an administration official testified in Congress in favor of this law. Nobody in America should be fired because they're gay, despite doing a great job and meeting their responsibilities. It's not fair. It's not right. We're going to put a stop to it. (Applause.) And it's for this reason that if any of my nominees are attacked not for what they believe but for who they are, I will not waver in my support, because I will not waver in my commitment to ending discrimination in all its forms. (Applause.)

We are reinvigorating our response to HIV/AIDS here at home and around the world. (Applause.) We're working closely with the Congress to renew the Ryan White program and I look forward to signing it into law in the very near future. (Applause.) We are rescinding the discriminatory ban on entry to the United States based on HIV status. (Applause.) The regulatory process to enact this important change is already underway. And we also know that HIV/AIDS continues to be a public health threat in many communities, including right here in the District of Columbia. Jeffrey Crowley, the Director of the Office of National AIDS Policy, recently held a forum in Washington, D.C., and is holding forums across the country, to seek input as we craft a national strategy to address this crisis.

We are moving ahead on Don't Ask Don't Tell. (Applause.) We should not be punishing patriotic Americans who have stepped forward to serve this country. We should be celebrating their willingness to show such courage and selflessness on behalf of their fellow citizens, especially when we're fighting two wars. (Applause.)

We cannot afford to cut from our ranks people with the critical skills we need to fight any more than we can afford — for our military's integrity — to force those willing to do so into careers encumbered and compromised by having to live a lie. So I'm working with the Pentagon, its leadership, and the members of the House and Senate on ending this policy. Legislation has been introduced in the House to make this happen. I will end Don't Ask, Don't Tell. That's my commitment to you. (Applause.)

It is no secret that issues of great concern to gays and lesbians are ones that raise a great deal of emotion in this country. And it's no secret that progress has been incredibly difficult — we can see that with the time and dedication it took to pass hate crimes legislation. But these issues also go to the heart of who we are as a people. Are we a nation that can transcend old attitudes and worn divides? Can we embrace our differences and look to the hopes and dreams that we share? Will we uphold the ideals on which this nation was founded: that all of us are equal, that all of us deserve the same opportunity to live our lives freely and pursue our chance at happiness? I believe we can; I believe we will. (Applause.)

And that is why — that's why I support ensuring that committed gay couples have the same rights and responsibilities afforded to any married couple in this country. (Applause.) I believe strongly in stopping laws designed to take rights away and passing laws that extend equal rights to gay couples. I've required all agencies in the federal government to extend as many federal benefits as possible to LGBT families as the current law allows. And I've called on Congress to repeal the so-called Defense of Marriage Act and to pass the Domestic Partners Benefits and Obligations Act. (Applause.) And we must all stand together against divisive and deceptive efforts to feed people's lingering fears for political and ideological gain.

For the struggle waged by the Human Rights Campaign is about more than any policy we can enshrine into law. It's about our capacity to love and commit to one another. It's about whether or not we value as a society that love and commitment. It's about our common humanity and our willingness to walk in someone else's shoes: to imagine losing a job not because of your performance at work but because of your relationship at home; to imagine worrying about a spouse in the hospital, with the added fear that you'll have to produce a legal document just to comfort the person you love — (applause) — to imagine the pain of losing a partner of decades and then discovering that the law treats you like a stranger. (Applause.)

If we are honest with ourselves we'll admit that there are too many who do not yet know in their lives or feel in their hearts the urgency of this struggle. That's why I continue to speak about the importance of equality for LGBT families — and not just in front of gay audiences. That's why Michelle and I have invited LGBT families to the White House to participate in events like the Easter Egg Roll — because we want to send a message. (Applause.) And that's why it's so important that you continue to speak out, that you continue to set an example, that you continue to pressure leaders — including me — and to make the case all across America. (Applause.)

So, tonight I'm hopeful — because of the activism I see in this room, because of the compassion I've seen all across America, and because of the progress we have made throughout our history, including the history of the movement for LGBT equality.

Soon after the protests at Stonewall 40 years ago, the phone rang in the home of a soft-spoken elementary school teacher named Jeanne Manford. It was 1:00 in the morning, and it was the police. Now, her son, Morty, had been at the Stonewall the night of the raids. Ever since, he had felt within him a new sense of purpose. So when the officer told Jeanne that her son had been arrested, which was happening often to gay protesters, she was not entirely caught off guard. And then the officer added one more thing, "And you know, he's homosexual." (Laughter.) Well, that police officer sure was surprised when Jeanne responded, "Yes, I know. Why are you bothering him?" (Applause.)

And not long after, Jeanne would be marching side-by-side with her son through the streets of New York. She carried a sign that stated her support. People cheered. Young men and women ran up to her, kissed her, and asked her to talk to their parents. And this gave Jeanne and Morty an idea.

And so, after that march on the anniversary of the Stonewall protests, amidst the violence and the vitriol of a difficult time for our nation, Jeanne and her husband Jules — two parents who loved their son deeply — formed a group to support other parents and, in turn, to support their children, as well. At the first meeting Jeanne held, in 1973, about 20 people showed up. But slowly, interest grew. Morty's life, tragically, was cut short by AIDS. But the cause endured. Today, the organization they founded for parents, families, and friends of lesbians and gays — (applause) — has more than 200,000 members and supporters, and has made a difference for countless families across America. And Jeanne would later say, "I considered myself such a traditional person. I didn't even cross the street against the light." (Laughter.) "But I wasn't going to let anybody walk over Morty." (Applause.)

That's the story of America: of ordinary citizens organizing, agitating and advocating for change; of hope stronger than hate; of love more powerful than any insult or injury; of Americans fighting to build for themselves and their families a nation in which no one is a second-class citizen, in which no one is denied their basic rights, in which all of us are free to live and love as we see fit. (Applause.)

Tonight, somewhere in America, a young person, let's say a young man, will struggle to fall to sleep, wrestling alone with a secret he's held as long as he can remember. Soon, perhaps, he will decide it's time to let that secret out. What happens next depends on him, his family, as well as his friends and his teachers and his community. But it also depends on us — on the kind of society we engender, the kind of future we build.

I believe the future is bright for that young person. For while there will be setbacks and bumps along the road, the truth is that our common ideals are a force far stronger than any division that some might sow. These ideals, when voiced by generations of citizens, are what made it possible for me to stand here today. (Applause.) These ideals are what made it possible for the people in this room to live freely and openly when for most of history that would have been inconceivable. That's the promise of America, HRC. That's the promise we're called to fulfill. (Applause.) Day by day, law by law, changing mind by mind, that is the promise we are fulfilling.

Thank you for the work you're doing. God bless you. God bless America. (Applause.)

Chapter 6

Remarks by the President at AAPI Initiative Executive Order Signing and Diwali Event

October 4, 2009

Well, good afternoon, everybody. Please be seated. Welcome to the White House. I'm glad you could join us today as I proudly sign this executive order reestablishing the President's Advisory Commission and White House Initiative on Asian American and Pacific Islanders.

Now, when we talk about America's AAPI communities, we're talking about the industry and entrepreneurship of people who've helped build this nation for centuries: from the early days, as laborers on our railroads and farmers tilling our land, to today, as leaders in every sector of American life, from business to science to academia, law and more.

We're talking about the creative energies of musicians like the singers Penn Masala — we appreciate them — who performed today. And we're talking about the competitive spirit of athletes like Wat Misaka, who played for the New York Knicks back in 1947 — the first non-white player in the NBA — and who served in the U.S. Army during World War II. Mr. Misaka is here as well today and — where's Mr. Misaka? There he is. Thank you so much. (Applause.)

We're talking about the public service of leaders like Secretaries Gary Locke and Steven Chu and Eric Shinseki and the folks on stage with me today. And we're talking about the courage and the patriotism and sacrifice of heroes like the members of the 442nd Regimental Combat Team who served in World War II, including Terry Shima. Please give him a big round of applause. (Applause.) Mr. Shima is the Executive Director of the Japanese American Veterans Association, and we are grateful that he took the time to be here today.

Some of their families had been interned. Some had been interned themselves. But they still insisted on fighting for America, and went on to become the most highly decorated unit of their size in history.

And one member of the regiment, Private Jake Kirihara, whose parents were held in a camp here in America while he fought overseas, later said: "... even though this wrong was done to us, there was never any question whether America was my country. If America needed me to help, I'll do it."

So this proud tradition of service continues today in Iraq and Afghanistan and around the world, carried on by folks like Tammy Duckworth, my dear friend who's here today. (Applause.) Tammy is a decorated member of our National Guard, a passionate advocate for our wounded warriors, who is now serving as our Assistant Secretary of Public and Intergovernmental Affairs at the Veterans Affairs Department. I'm proud to have her on board and pleased that she could join us today.

And on a personal note, when I talk about America's AAPI communities, I'm talking about my own family: my sister, Maya; my brother-in-law, Konrad; my beautiful nieces, Suhaila and Savita; and the folks I grew up with in Indonesia, and in Honolulu, as part of the Hawai'ian Ohana, or family.

Our AAPI communities have roots that span the globe, but they embody a rich diversity, and a story of striving and success that are uniquely American.

But focusing on all of these achievements doesn't tell the whole story, and that's part of why we're here. It's tempting, given the strengths of the Asian American and Pacific Islander communities, for us to buy into the myth of the "model minority," and to overlook the very real challenges that certain Asian American and Pacific Islander communities are facing: from health disparities like higher rates of diabetes and Hepatitis B; to educational disparities that still exist in some communities — high dropout rates, low college enrollment rates; to economic disparities — higher rates of poverty in some communities, and barriers to employment and workplace advancement in others.

Some Asian American and Pacific Islanders, particularly new Americans and refugees, still face language barriers. Others have been victims of unthinkable hate crimes, particularly in the months after September 11th — crimes driven by ignorance and prejudice that are an affront to everything that this nation stands for.

And then there are the disparities that we don't even know about because our data collection methods still aren't up to par. Too often, Asian American and Pacific Islanders are all lumped into one category, so we don't have accurate numbers reflecting the challenges of each individual community. Smaller communities in particular can get lost, their needs and concerns buried in a spreadsheet.

And that's why I'm signing this executive order today, reestablishing the advisory commission and White House initiative created by President Clinton 10 years ago. Because when any of our citizens — (applause) — when any of our citizens are unable to fulfill their potential due to factors that have nothing to do with their talent, character, or work ethic, then I believe there's a role for our government to play. Not to guarantee anybody's success or to solve everybody's problems, but to ensure that we're living up to our nation's ideals; to ensure that we can each pursue our own version of happiness, and that we continue to be a nation where all things are still possible for all people. That's the impact that our government can have.

It's the impact of a Small Business Administration that offers loans to Asian American and Pacific Islander entrepreneurs whose small businesses sustain so many communities around the country. It's the impact of a Department of Health and Human Services that funds research on the diseases that disproportionately affect Asian American and Pacific Islander families. It's the impact of a Justice Department that upholds the Voting Rights Act and its promise of language assistance and equal access to the polls. And it's the impact of evidence-based research and data collection and analysis on AAPI communities — so that no one is invisible to their government.

All of that is the mission of this initiative and commission — to work with 23 agencies and departments across our government to improve the health, education, and economic status of AAPI communities. The initiative and commission will be housed in the Department of Education, and they'll be co-chaired by Secretaries Arne Duncan and Secretary Gary Locke, both of whom have devoted their lives to promoting opportunity for all our citizens.

And I think it's fitting that we begin this work in the week leading up to the holiday of Diwali — the festival of lights — when members of some of the world's greatest faiths celebrate the triumph of good over evil.

This coming Saturday, Hindus, Jains, Sikhs and some Buddhists, here in America and around the world, will celebrate this holiday by lighting Diyas, or lamps, which symbolize the victory of light over darkness, and knowledge over ignorance. And while this is a time of rejoicing, it's also a time for reflection, when we remember those who are less fortunate and renew our commitment to reach out to those in need.

While the significance of the holiday for each faith varies, all of them mark it by gathering with family members to pray and decorate the house and enjoy delicious food and sweet treats. And in that spirit of celebration and contemplation, I am happy to light the White House Diya, and wish you all a Happy Diwali, and a Saal Mubarak. (Applause.)

Chapter 7

Remarks by the President at Reception Commemorating the Enactment of the Matthew Shepard and James Byrd, Jr. Hate Crimes Prevention Act

October 28, 2009

Thank you so much, everybody. Thank you so much, and welcome to the White House.

There are several people here that I want to just make mention of because they helped to make today possible. We've got Attorney General Eric Holder. (Applause.) A champion of this legislation, and a great Speaker of the House, Nancy Pelosi. (Applause.) My dear friend, senior Senator from the great state of Illinois, Dick Durbin. (Applause.) The outstanding Chairman of Armed Services, Carl Levin. (Applause.) Senator Arlen Specter. (Applause.) Chairman of the Judiciary Committee in the House, Representative John Conyers. (Applause.) Representative Barney Frank. (Applause.) Representative Tammy Baldwin. (Applause.) Representative Jerry Nadler. (Applause.) Representative Jared Polis. (Applause.) All the members of Congress who are here today, we thank you.

Mr. David Bohnett and Mr. Tom Gregory and the David Bohnett Foundation — they are partners for this reception. Thank you so much, guys, for helping to host this. (Applause.)

And finally, and most importantly, because these were really the spearheads of this effort — Denis, Judy, and Logan Shepard. (Applause.) As well as Betty Byrd Boatner and Louvon Harris — sisters of James Byrd, Jr. (Applause.)

To all the activists, all the organizers, all the people who helped make this day happen, thank you for your years of advocacy and activism, pushing and protesting that made this victory possible.

You know, as a nation we've come far on the journey towards a more perfect union. And today, we've taken another step forward. This afternoon, I signed into law the Matthew Shepard and James Byrd, Jr. Hate Crimes Prevention Act. (Applause.)

This is the culmination of a struggle that has lasted more than a decade. Time and again, we faced opposition. Time and again, the measure was defeated or delayed. Time and again we've been reminded of the difficulty of building a nation in which we're all free to live and love as we see fit. But the cause endured and the struggle continued, waged by the family of Matthew Shepard, by the family of James Byrd, by folks who held vigils and led marches, by those who rallied and organized and refused to give up, by the late Senator Ted Kennedy who fought so hard for this legislation — (applause) — and all who toiled for years to reach this day.

You understood that we must stand against crimes that are meant not only to break bones, but to break spirits — not only to inflict harm, but to instill fear. You understand that the rights afforded every citizen under our Constitution mean nothing if we do not protect those rights — both from unjust laws and violent acts. And you understand how necessary this law continues to be.

In the most recent year for which we have data, the FBI reported roughly 7,600 hate crimes in this country. Over the past 10 years, there were more than 12,000 reported hate crimes based on sexual orientation alone. And we will never know how many incidents were never reported at all.

And that's why, through this law, we will strengthen the protections against crimes based on the color of your skin, the faith in your heart, or the place of your birth. We will finally add federal protections against crimes based on gender, disability, gender identity, or sexual orientation. (Applause.) And prosecutors will have new tools to work with states in order to prosecute to the fullest those who would perpetrate such crimes. Because no one in America should ever be afraid to walk down the street holding the hands of the person they love. No one in America should be forced to look over their shoulder because of who they are or because they live with a disability.

At root, this isn't just about our laws; this is about who we are as a people. This is about whether we value one another — whether we embrace our differences, rather than allowing them to become a source of animus. It's hard for any of us to imagine the mind-set of someone who would kidnap a young man and beat him to within an inch of his life, tie him to a fence, and leave him for dead. It's hard for any of us to imagine the twisted mentality of those who'd offer a neighbor a ride home, attack him, chain him to the back of a truck, and drag him for miles until he finally died.

But we sense where such cruelty begins: the moment we fail to see in another our common humanity — the very moment when we fail to recognize in a person the same fears and hopes, the same passions and imperfections, the same dreams that we all share.

We have for centuries strived to live up to our founding ideal, of a nation where all are free and equal and able to pursue their own version of happiness. Through conflict and tumult, through the morass of hatred and prejudice, through periods of division and discord we have endured and grown stronger and fairer and freer. And at every turn, we've made progress not only by changing laws but by changing hearts, by our willingness to walk in another's shoes, by our capacity to love and accept even in the face of rage and bigotry.

In April of 1968, just one week after the assassination of Martin Luther King, as our nation mourned in grief and shuddered in anger, President Lyndon Johnson signed landmark civil rights legislation. This was the first time we enshrined into law federal protections against crimes motivated by religious or racial hatred — the law on which we build today.

As he signed his name, at a difficult moment for our country, President Johnson said that through this law "the bells of freedom ring out a little louder." That is the promise of America. Over the sounds of hatred and chaos, over the din of grief and anger, we can still hear those ideals — even when they are faint, even when some would try to drown them out. At our best we seek to make sure those ideals can be heard and felt by Americans everywhere. And that work did not end in 1968. It certainly does not end today. But because of the efforts of the folks in this room — particularly those family members who are standing behind me — we can be proud that that bell rings even louder now and each day grows louder still.

So thank you very much. God bless you and God bless the United States of America. (Applause.)

Chapter 8

Remarks by the President in Remembrance of Dr. Martin Luther King, Jr.

January 17, 2010

Good morning. Praise be to God. Let me begin by thanking the entire Vermont Avenue Baptist Church family for welcoming our family here today. It feels like a family. Thank you for making us feel that way. (Applause.) To Pastor Wheeler, first lady Wheeler, thank you so much for welcoming us here today. Congratulations on Jordan Denice — aka Cornelia. (Laughter.)

Michelle and I have been blessed with a new nephew this year as well — Austin Lucas Robinson. (Applause.) So maybe at the appropriate time we can make introductions. (Laughter.) Now, if Jordan's father is like me, then that will be in about 30 years. (Laughter.) That is a great blessing.

Michelle and Malia and Sasha and I are thrilled to be here today. And I know that sometimes you have to go through a little fuss to have me as a guest speaker. (Laughter.) So let me apologize in advance for all the fuss.

We gather here, on a Sabbath, during a time of profound difficulty for our nation and for our world. In such a time, it soothes the soul to seek out the Divine in a spirit of prayer; to seek solace among a community of believers. But we are not here just to ask the Lord for His blessing. We aren't here just to interpret His Scripture. We're also here to call on the memory of one of His noble servants, the Reverend Dr.

Martin Luther King, Jr.

Now, it's fitting that we do so here, within the four walls of Vermont Avenue Baptist Church — here, in a church that rose like the phoenix from the ashes of the civil war; here in a church formed by freed slaves, whose founding pastor had worn the union blue; here in a church from whose pews congregants set out for marches and from whom choir anthems of freedom were heard; from whose sanctuary King himself would sermonize from time to time.

One of those times was Thursday, December 6, 1956. Pastor, you said you were a little older than me, so were you around at that point? (Laughter.) You were three years old — okay. (Laughter.) I wasn't born yet. (Laughter.)   On Thursday, December 6, 1956. And before Dr. King had pointed us to the mountaintop, before he told us about his dream in front of the Lincoln Memorial, King came here, as a 27-year-old preacher, to speak on what he called "The Challenge of a New Age." "The Challenge of a New Age." It was a period of triumph, but also uncertainty, for Dr. King and his followers — because just weeks earlier, the Supreme Court had ordered the desegregation of Montgomery's buses, a hard-wrought, hard-fought victory that would put an end to the 381-day historic boycott down in Montgomery, Alabama.

And yet, as Dr. King rose to take that pulpit, the future still seemed daunting. It wasn't clear what would come next for the movement that Dr. King led. It wasn't clear how we were going to reach the Promised Land. Because segregation was still rife; lynchings still a fact. Yes, the Supreme Court had ruled not only on the Montgomery buses, but also on Brown v. Board of Education. And yet that ruling was defied throughout the South — by schools and by states; they ignored it with impunity. And here in the nation's capital, the federal government had yet to fully align itself with the laws on its books and the ideals of its founding.

So it's not hard for us, then, to imagine that moment. We can imagine folks coming to this church, happy about the boycott being over. We can also imagine them, though, coming here concerned about their future, sometimes second-guessing strategy, maybe fighting off some creeping doubts, perhaps despairing about whether the movement in which they had placed so many of their hopes — a movement in which they believed so deeply — could actually deliver on its promise.

So here we are, more than half a century later, once again facing the challenges of a new age. Here we are, once more marching toward an unknown future, what I call the Joshua generation to their Moses generation — the great inheritors of progress paid for with sweat and blood, and sometimes life itself.

We've inherited the progress of unjust laws that are now overturned. We take for granted the progress of a ballot being available to anybody who wants to take the time to actually vote. We enjoy the fruits of prejudice and bigotry being lifted — slowly, sometimes in fits and starts, but irrevocably — from human hearts. It's that progress that made it possible for me to be here today; for the good people of this country to elect an African American the 44th President of the United States of America.

Reverend Wheeler mentioned the inauguration, last year's election. You know, on the heels of that victory over a year ago, there were some who suggested that somehow we had entered into a post-racial America, all those problems would be solved. There were those who argued that because I had spoke of a need for unity in this country that our nation was somehow entering into a period of post-partisanship. That didn't work out so well. There was a hope shared by many that life would be better from the moment that I swore that oath.

Of course, as we meet here today, one year later, we know the promise of that moment has not yet been fully fulfilled. Because of an era of greed and irresponsibility that sowed the seeds of its own demise, because of persistent economic troubles unaddressed through the generations, because of a banking crisis that brought the financial system to the brink of catastrophe, we are being tested — in our own lives and as a nation — as few have been tested before.

Unemployment is at its highest level in more than a quarter of a century. Nowhere is it higher than the African American community. Poverty is on the rise. Home ownership is slipping. Beyond our shores, our sons and daughters are fighting two wars. Closer to home, our Haitian brothers and sisters are in desperate need. Bruised, battered, many people are legitimately feeling doubt, even despair, about the future. Like those who came to this church on that Thursday in 1956, folks are wondering, where do we go from here?

I understand those feelings. I understand the frustration and some-times anger that so many folks feel as they struggle to stay afloat. I get letters from folks around the country every day; I read 10 a night out of the 40,000 that we receive. And there are stories of hardship and desperation, in some cases, pleading for help: I need a job. I'm about to lose my home. I don't have health care — it's about to cause my family to be bankrupt. Sometimes you get letters from children: My mama or my daddy have lost their jobs, is there something you can do to help? Ten letters like that a day we read.

So, yes, we're passing through a hard winter. It's the hardest in some time. But let's always remember that, as a people, the American people, we've weathered some hard winters before. This country was founded during some harsh winters. The fishermen, the laborers, the craftsmen who made camp at Valley Forge — they weathered a hard winter. The slaves and the freedmen who rode an underground railroad, seeking the light of justice under the cover of night — they weathered a hard winter. The seamstress whose feet were tired, the pastor whose voice echoes through the ages — they weathered some hard winters. It was for them, as it is for us, difficult, in the dead of winter, to sometimes see spring coming. They, too, sometimes felt their hopes deflate. And yet, each season, the frost melts, the cold recedes, the sun reappears. So it was for earlier generations and so it will be for us.

What we need to do is to just ask what lessons we can learn from those earlier generations about how they sustained themselves during those hard winters, how they persevered and prevailed. Let us in this Joshua generation learn how that Moses generation overcame.

Let me offer a few thoughts on this. First and foremost, they did so by remaining firm in their resolve. Despite being threatened by sniper fire or planted bombs, by shoving and punching and spitting and angry stares, they adhered to that sweet spirit of resistance, the principles of nonviolence that had accounted for their success.

Second, they understood that as much as our government and our political parties had betrayed them in the past — as much as our na-tion itself had betrayed its own ideals — government, if aligned with the interests of its people, can be — and must be — a force for good. So they stayed on the Justice Department. They went into the courts. They pressured Congress, they pressured their President. They didn't give up on this country. They didn't give up on government. They didn't somehow say government was the problem; they said, we're going to change government, we're going to make it better. Imperfect as it was, they continued to believe in the promise of democracy; in America's constant ability to remake itself, to perfect this union.

Third, our predecessors were never so consumed with theoretical debates that they couldn't see progress when it came. Sometimes I get a little frustrated when folks just don't want to see that even if we don't get everything, we're getting something. (Applause.) King understood that the desegregation of the Armed Forces didn't end the civil rights movement, because black and white soldiers still couldn't sit together at the same lunch counter when they came home. But he still insisted on the rightness of desegregating the Armed Forces. That was a good first step — even as he called for more. He didn't suggest that somehow by the signing of the Civil Rights that somehow all discrimination would end. But he also didn't think that we shouldn't sign the Civil Rights Act because it hasn't solved every problem. Let's take a victory, he said, and then keep on marching. Forward steps, large and small, were recognized for what they were — which was progress.

Fourth, at the core of King's success was an appeal to conscience that touched hearts and opened minds, a commitment to universal ideals — of freedom, of justice, of equality — that spoke to all people, not just some people. For King understood that without broad support, any movement for civil rights could not be sustained. That's why he marched with the white auto worker in Detroit. That's why he linked arm with the Mexican farm worker in California, and united people of all colors in the noble quest for freedom.

Of course, King overcame in other ways as well. He remained strategically focused on gaining ground — his eyes on the prize constantly — understanding that change would not be easy, understand that change wouldn't come overnight, understanding that there would be setbacks and false starts along the way, but understanding, as he said in 1956, that "we can walk and never get weary, because we know there is a great camp meeting in the promised land of freedom and justice."

And it's because the Moses generation overcame that the trials we face today are very different from the ones that tested us in previous generations. Even after the worst recession in generations, life in America is not even close to being as brutal as it was back then for so many. That's the legacy of Dr. King and his movement. That's our inheritance. Having said that, let there be no doubt the challenges of our new age are serious in their own right, and we must face them as squarely as they faced the challenges they saw.

I know it's been a hard road we've traveled this year to rescue the economy, but the economy is growing again. The job losses have finally slowed, and around the country, there's signs that businesses and families are beginning to rebound. We are making progress.

I know it's been a hard road that we've traveled to reach this point on health reform. I promise you I know. (Laughter.) But under the legislation I will sign into law, insurance companies won't be able to drop you when you get sick, and more than 30 million people — (applause) — our fellow Americans will finally have insurance. More than 30 million men and women and children, mothers and fathers, won't be worried about what might happen to them if they get sick. This will be a victory not for Democrats; this will be a victory for dignity and decency, for our common humanity. This will be a victory for the United States of America.

Let's work to change the political system, as imperfect as it is. I know people can feel down about the way things are going sometimes here in Washington. I know it's tempting to give up on the political process. But we've put in place tougher rules on lobbying and ethics and transparency — tougher rules than any administration in history. It's not enough, but it's progress. Progress is possible. Don't give up on voting. Don't give up on advocacy. Don't give up on activism. There are too many needs to be met, too much work to be done. Like Dr. King said, "We must accept finite disappointment but never lose infinite hope."

Let us broaden our coalition, building a confederation not of liberals or conservatives, not of red states or blue states, but of all Americans who are hurting today, and searching for a better tomorrow. The urgency of the hour demands that we make common cause with all of America's workers — white, black, brown — all of whom are being hammered by this recession, all of whom are yearning for that spring to come. It demands that we reach out to those who've been left out in the cold even when the economy is good, even when we're not in recession — the youth in the inner cities, the youth here in Washington, D.C., people in rural communities who haven't seen prosperity reach them for a very long time. It demands that we fight discrimination, whatever form it may come. That means we fight discrimination against gays and lesbians, and we make common cause to reform our immigration system. And finally, we have to recognize, as Dr. King did, that progress can't just come from without — it also has to come from within. And over the past year, for example, we've made meaningful improvements in the field of education. I've got a terrific Secretary of Education, Arne Duncan. He's been working hard with states and working hard with the D.C. school district, and we've insisted on reform, and we've insisted on accountability. We we're putting in more money and we've provided more Pell Grants and more tuition tax credits and simpler financial aid forms. We've done all that, but parents still need to parent. (Applause.) Kids still need to own up to their responsibilities. We still have to set high expectations for our young people. Folks can't simply look to government for all the answers without also looking inside themselves, inside their own homes, for some of the answers.

Progress will only come if we're willing to promote that ethic of hard work, a sense of responsibility, in our own lives. I'm not talking, by the way, just to the African American community. Sometimes when I say these things people assme, well, he's just talking to black people about working hard. No, no, no, no. I'm talking to the American community. Because somewhere along the way, we, as a nation, began to lose touch with some of our core values. You know what I'm talking about. We became enraptured with the false prophets who prophesized an easy path to success, paved with credit cards and home equity loans and get-rich-quick schemes, and the most important thing was to be a celebrity; it doesn't matter what you do, as long as you get on TV. That's everybody.

We forgot what made the bus boycott a success; what made the civil rights movement a success; what made the United States of America a success — that, in this country, there's no substitute for hard work, no substitute for a job well done, no substitute for being responsible stewards of God's blessings.

What we're called to do, then, is rebuild America from its foundation on up. To reinvest in the essentials that we've neglected for too long — like health care, like education, like a better energy policy, like basic infrastructure, like scientific research. Our generation is called to buckle down and get back to basics.

We must do so not only for ourselves, but also for our children, and their children. For Jordan and for Austin. That's a sacrifice that falls on us to make. It's a much smaller sacrifice than the Moses generation had to make, but it's still a sacrifice.

Yes, it's hard to transition to a clean energy economy. Sometimes it may be inconvenient, but it's a sacrifice that we have to make. It's hard to be fiscally responsible when we have all these human needs, and we're inheriting enormous deficits and debt, but that's a sacrifice that we're going to have to make. You know, it's easy, after a hard day's work, to just put your kid in front of the TV set — you're tired, don't want to fuss with them — instead of reading to them, but that's a sacrifice we must joyfully accept.

Sometimes it's hard to be a good father and good mother. Sometimes it's hard to be a good neighbor, or a good citizen, to give up time in service of others, to give something of ourselves to a cause that's greater than ourselves — as Michelle and I are urging folks to do tomorrow to honor and celebrate Dr. King. But these are sacrifices that we are called to make. These are sacrifices that our faith calls us to make. Our faith in the future. Our faith in America. Our faith in God.

And on his sermon all those years ago, Dr. King quoted a poet's verse:

Truth forever on the scaffold Wrong forever on the throne... And behind the dim unknown stands God Within the shadows keeping watch above his own.

Even as Dr. King stood in this church, a victory in the past and uncertainty in the future, he trusted God. He trusted that God would make a way. A way for prayers to be answered. A way for our union to be perfected. A way for the arc of the moral universe, no matter how long, to slowly bend towards truth and bend towards freedom, to bend towards justice. He had faith that God would make a way out of no way.

You know, folks ask me sometimes why I look so calm. (Laughter.) They say, all this stuff coming at you, how come you just seem calm? And I have a confession to make here. There are times where I'm not so calm. (Laughter.) Reggie Love knows. My wife knows. There are times when progress seems too slow. There are times when the words that are spoken about me hurt. There are times when the barbs sting. There are times when it feels like all these efforts are for naught, and change is so painfully slow in coming, and I have to confront my own doubts.

But let me tell you — during those times it's faith that keeps me calm. (Applause.) It's faith that gives me peace. The same faith that leads a single mother to work two jobs to put a roof over her head when she has doubts. The same faith that keeps an unemployed father to keep on submitting job applications even after he's been rejected a hundred times. The same faith that says to a teacher even if the first nine children she's teaching she can't reach, that that 10th one she's going to be able to reach. The same faith that breaks the silence of an earthquake's wake with the sound of prayers and hymns sung by a Haitian community. A faith in things not seen, in better days ahead, in Him who holds the future in the hollow of His hand. A faith that lets us mount up on wings like eagles; lets us run and not be weary; lets us walk and not faint.

So let us hold fast to that faith, as Joshua held fast to the faith of his fathers, and together, we shall overcome the challenges of a new age. (Applause.) Together, we shall seize the promise of this moment. Together, we shall make a way through winter, and we're going to welcome the spring. Through God all things are possible. (Applause.)

May the memory of Dr. Martin Luther King continue to inspire us and ennoble our world and all who inhabit it. And may God bless the United States of America. Thank you very much, everybody. God bless you. (Applause.)

Chapter 9

Remarks by the President Following Intergenerational Reflection on the Civil Rights Movement

January 18, 2010

Hello, everybody. We have just had a wonderful conversation. I want to just tell you a little bit about why we did this. I think sometimes in celebration of Dr. King's birthday we act as if this history was so long ago.

And the reason we brought together some elders and some young people very briefly was not just to visit the Oval Office and see the Emancipation Proclamation, which is going to be on loan to us, but it's also just to remind us that there were some extraordinarily courageous young people like Dr. Dorothy Height, like Mrs. Eleanor Banks and Romaine Thomas and her husband, and others who were actively involved in bringing about one of the great moments in United States history.

And so what we've done is we've heard some stories, shared — Dr. Height has shared with us what it was like meeting Martin Luther King when he was a 15-year-old at Morehouse, visiting there. We heard from Ms. Glanton, Willie Glanton, who is a great activist in Iowa, about the work that she's done there on behalf of the civil rights movement, reminding us that it wasn't just isolated in some areas.

I am especially proud to have the Harveys here — Mr. Joseph Harvey and Ms. Mabel Harvey. Mr. Joseph Harvey is 105, and Ms. Mabel Harvey here is the spry young one at 102. (Laughter.) And Ms. Harvey just now was whispering in my ear, as you guys were walking in, that this must be the Lord's doing, because we've come a mighty long way. (Laughter.) That's what she said. And so that's wonderful to hear.

We've heard from some young people who were sharing in these stories and understanding that this is a living history. And I was very pleased to hear from Taylor Branch, author of one of the definitive biographies of the civil rights movement and Dr. King. He shared, I thought, a really interesting idea, which is that not only is Dr. King's birthday a time to celebrate service, to reflect and study on how we had helped to perfect our union, but that it should be a day in which each of us individually also try to stretch out of our comfort zones and try to do something for others and to reach out and learn about things that maybe we've shied away from — because part of what the civil rights movement was all about was changing people's hearts and minds and breaking out of old customs and old habits.

That's, I think, an important lesson for all of us on this day — are the things that we can try to do that might have seemed impossible but we know are worth doing, and can we apply those principles that we know to be true in our own lives and our society.

So I'm just so grateful that we had this opportunity to share with everybody. And I want to wish everybody around the country a day in which they reflect on the extraordinary contributions that ordinary people can make each and every day to make America the most hopeful country in the world.

Thank you very much, everybody.

Chapter 10

Remarks by the President at "In Performance at the White House: A Celebration of Music from the Civil Rights Movement"

February 10, 2010

Welcome to the White House, everybody. And thank you for braving the storm. I am thrilled to see all of you here today — friends, guests, members of my Cabinet, members of Congress, our Vice President and Dr. Jill Biden, and everyone watching at home — for the fifth in a series of evenings celebrating the music that tells the story of America.

Tonight, we celebrate the music of a movement.

To help us do that, Michelle and I are thrilled to welcome a tremendous group of artists who influenced that music, and artists who were influenced by it:

Yolanda Adams; Joan Baez; Natalie Cole; Morgan Freeman; Jennifer Hudson; John Mellencamp; Dr. Bernice Johnson Reagon; Smokey Robinson; the Blind Boys of Alabama; the Howard University Choir; and a man who was good enough to take a night off from his Never Ending Tour — Mr. Bob Dylan.

I want to thank some of them for spending some time earlier here today, leading a workshop of high school students — perhaps even inspiring the next generation of civil rights leaders.

Let me also just acknowledge a good friend to us all, Dr. Joseph Lowery, who was here — who couldn't be here with us today, but he is recuperating after an illness and we want to keep him in our thoughts and prayers tonight.

Now, the civil rights movement was a movement sustained by music. It was lifted by spirituals inspired by the Bible. It was sharpened by protest songs about wrongs that needed righting. It was broadened by folk artists like a New York-born daughter of immigrants, and a young storyteller from Minnesota, who captured the hardships and hopes of people who were worlds different from them, in ways that only song can do.

It was a movement with a soundtrack — diverse strains of music that coalesced when the moment was right. But that soundtrack wasn't just inspired by the movement; it gave strength in return — a fact not lost on the movement's leaders.

It's been said that when Dr. King and his associates were looking for communities to organize and mobilize, they'd know which were disciplined enough and serious enough when they saw folks singing freedom songs. Dr. King himself once acknowledged that he didn't see "the real meaning of the movement" until he saw young people singing in the face of hostility.

You see, it's easy to sing when you're happy. It's easy to sing when you're among friends. It's easy to sing when times are good. But it is hard to sing when times are rough. It's hard to sing in the face of taunts, and fear, and the constant threat of violence. It's hard to sing when folks are being beaten, when leaders are being jailed, when churches are being bombed.

It's hard to sing in times like that. But times like that are precisely when the power of song is most potent. Above the din of hatred; amidst the deafening silence of inaction; the hymns of the civil rights movement helped carry the cause of a people and advance the ideals of a nation.

Bernice Johnson Reagon knew this. One day when she was young, she was sitting in church when a local sheriff and his deputies showed up to intimidate the congregation. "They stood at the door," Bernice wrote, "making sure everyone knew they were there. Then," she said;

"a song began. And the song made sure that the sheriff and his deputies knew that we were there."

Joan Baez and Bob Dylan knew this. One day in 1963, they joined hundreds of thousands on the National Mall and sang of a day when the time would come; when the winds would stop; when a ship would come in. They sang of a day when a righteous journey would reach its destination.

And Congressman John Lewis — a man of that Moses Generation; a man who couldn't be here tonight, but whose sacrifices helped make it possible for me to be here tonight — he knew this too. For in the darkest hour, he said, "the songs fed our spirits and gave us hope."

So to everyone here, or watching at home, let us enjoy the music we hear tonight. Let the music feed our spirits; give us hope; and carry us forward — as one people, and as one nation. Enjoy. (Applause.)

Chapter 11

Remarks by the President at Funeral Service for Dr. Dorothy Height

April 29, 2010

Let me begin by saying a word to Dr. Dorothy Height's sister, Ms. Aldridge. To some, she was a mentor. To all, she was a friend. But to you, she was family, and my family offers yours our sympathy for your loss.

We are gathered here today to celebrate the life, and mourn the passing, of Dr. Dorothy Height. It is fitting that we do so here, in our National Cathedral of Saint Peter and Saint Paul. Here, in a place of great honor. Here, in the House of God. Surrounded by the love of family and of friends. The love in this sanctuary is a testament to a life lived righteously; a life that lifted other lives; a life that changed this country for the better over the course of nearly one century here on Earth.

Michelle and I didn't know Dr. Height as well, or as long, as many of you. We were reminded during a previous moment in the service, when you have a nephew who's 88 — (laughter) — you've lived a full life. (Applause.)

But we did come to know her in the early days of my campaign. And we came to love her, as so many loved her. We came to love her stories. And we loved her smile. And we loved those hats — (laughter) — that she wore like a crown — regal. In the White House, she was a regular. She came by not once, not twice — 21 times she stopped by the White House. (Laughter and applause.) Took part in our discussions around health care reform in her final months.

Last February, I was scheduled to see her and other civil rights leaders to discuss the pressing problems of unemployment — Reverend Sharpton, Ben Jealous of the NAACP, Marc Morial of the National Urban League. Then we discovered that Washington was about to be blanketed by the worst blizzard in record — two feet of snow.

So I suggested to one of my aides, we should call Dr. Height and say we're happy to reschedule the meeting. Certainly if the others come, she should not feel obliged. True to form, Dr. Height insisted on coming, despite the blizzard, never mind that she was in a wheelchair. She was not about to let just a bunch of men — (laughter) — in this meeting. (Applause.) It was only when the car literally could not get to her driveway that she reluctantly decided to stay home. But she still sent a message — (laughter) — about what needed to be done.

And I tell that story partly because it brings a smile to my face, but also because it captures the quiet, dogged, dignified persistence that all of us who loved Dr. Height came to know so well — an attribute that we understand she learned early on.

Born in the capital of the old Confederacy, brought north by her parents as part of that great migration, Dr. Height was raised in another age, in a different America, beyond the experience of many. It's hard to imagine, I think, life in the first decades of that last century when the elderly woman that we knew was only a girl. Jim Crow ruled the South. The Klan was on the rise — a powerful political force. Lynching was all too often the penalty for the offense of black skin. Slaves had been freed within living memory, but too often, their children, their grandchildren remained captive, because they were denied justice and denied equality, denied opportunity, denied a chance to pursue their dreams.

The progress that followed — progress that so many of you helped to achieve, progress that ultimately made it possible for Michelle and me to be here as President and First Lady — that progress came slowly. (Applause.)

Progress came from the collective effort of multiple generations of Americans. From preachers and lawyers, and thinkers and doers, men and women like Dr. Height, who took it upon themselves — often at great risk — to change this country for the better. From men like W.E.B

Du Bois and A. Philip Randolph; women like Mary McLeod Bethune and Betty Friedan — they're Americans whose names we know. They are leaders whose legacies we teach. They are giants who fill our history books. Well, Dr. Dorothy Height deserves a place in this pantheon. She, too, deserves a place in our history books. (Applause.) She, too, deserves a place of honor in America's memory.

Look at her body of work. Desegregating the YWCA. Laying the groundwork for integration on Wednesdays in Mississippi. Lending pigs to poor farmers as a sustainable source of income. Strategizing with civil rights leaders, holding her own, the only woman in the room, Queen Esther to this Moses Generation — even as she led the National Council of Negro Women with vision and energy — (applause) — with vision and energy, vision and class.

But we remember her not solely for all she did during the civil rights movement. We remember her for all she did over a lifetime, behind the scenes, to broaden the movement's reach. To shine a light on stable families and tight-knit communities. To make us see the drive for civil rights and women's rights not as a separate struggle, but as part of a larger movement to secure the rights of all humanity, regardless of gender, regardless of race, regardless of ethnicity.

It's an unambiguous record of righteous work, worthy of remembrance, worthy of recognition. And yet, one of the ironies is, is that year after year, decade in, decade out, Dr. Height went about her work quietly, without fanfare, without self-promotion. She never cared about who got the credit. She didn't need to see her picture in the papers. She understood that the movement gathered strength from the bottom up, those unheralded men and women who don't always make it into the history books but who steadily insisted on their dignity, on their manhood and womanhood. (Applause.) She wasn't interested in credit. What she cared about was the cause. The cause of justice. The cause of equality. The cause of opportunity. Freedom's cause.

And that willingness to subsume herself, that humility and that grace, is why we honor Dr. Dorothy Height. As it is written in the Gospel of Matthew: "For whoever exalts himself will be humbled, and whoever humbles himself will be exalted." I don't think the author of the Gospel would mind me rephrasing: "whoever humbles herself will be exalted." (Applause.)

One of my favorite moments with Dr. Height — this was just a few months ago — we had decided to put up the Emancipation Proclamation in the Oval Office, and we invited some elders to share reflections of the movement. And she came and it was a inter-generational event, so we had young children there, as well as elders, and the elders were asked to share stories. And she talked about attending a dinner in the 1940s at the home of Dr. Benjamin Mays, then president of Morehouse College. And seated at the table that evening was a 15-year-old student, "a gifted child," as she described him, filled with a sense of purpose, who was trying to decide whether to enter medicine, or law, or the ministry.

And many years later, after that gifted child had become a gifted preacher — I'm sure he had been told to be on his best behavior — after he led a bus boycott in Montgomery, and inspired a nation with his dreams, he delivered a sermon on what he called "the drum major instinct" — a sermon that said we all have the desire to be first, we all want to be at the front of the line.

The great test of a life, Dr. Martin Luther King Jr. said, is to harness that instinct; to redirect it towards advancing the greater good; toward changing a community and a country for the better; toward doing the Lord's work.

I sometimes think Dr. King must have had Dorothy Height in mind when he gave that speech. For Dorothy Height met the test. Dorothy Height embodied that instinct. Dorothy Height was a drum major for justice. A drum major for equality. A drum major for freedom. A drum major for service. And the lesson she would want us to leave with today — a lesson she lived out each and every day — is that we can all be first in service. We can all be drum majors for a righteous cause. So let us live out that lesson. Let us honor her life by changing this country for the better as long as we are blessed to live. May God bless Dr. Dorothy Height and the union that she made more perfect. (Applause.)

Chapter 12

Remarks by the President Before Signing the Tribal Law and Order Act

July 29, 2010

I want to start, obviously, by thanking Lisa for her introduction and having the courage to share her story with all of us today. It's for every survivor like Lisa who has never gotten their day in court, and for every family that feels like justice is beyond reach, and for every tribal community struggling to keep its people safe, that I'll be signing the Tribal Law and Order Act into law today.

And in doing so, I intend to send a clear message that all of our people — whether they live in our biggest cities or our most remote reservations — have the right to feel safe in their own communities, and to raise their children in peace, and enjoy the fullest protection of our laws.

As many of you know, I campaigned on this issue. And during our last — during our tribal conference last year, I pledged my administration's fullest support for this bill. And I told Senator Dorgan last week that I intended to sign it in a ceremony here at the White House with all of you. So today, I am proud to make good on my word.

Now, I'm told there's a Seneca proverb that says "He who would do great things should not attempt them all alone." (Laughter.) And that's particularly true of this legislation, which is the product of tireless efforts by countless individuals across this country. Congressional leaders like Senator Dorgan, Representative Herseth Sandlin, and others who are here today, and tribal leaders like Chairman Marcus Levings, President Theresa Two Bulls, President Diane Enos, Chief Chad Smith, Vice Chairman Jonathan Windy Boy — we are grateful to all of them for their extraordinary support. And then we've got leaders in our administration like Attorney General Holder and Secretary Salazar, Kimberly Teehee, Jodi Gillette here at the White House who work tirelessly on this legislation.

And that's nothing to say of all the dedicated judges and prosecutors and tribal and BIA law enforcement officers — some of whom are here today — who've supported these efforts. And the determined survivors most of all, like Lisa, who even when it's too late to undo what happened to them, still speak out to seek justice for others.

All of you come at this from different angles, but you're united in support of this bill because you believe, like I do, that it is unconscionable that crime rates in Indian Country are more than twice the national average and up to 20 times the national average on some reservations. And all of you believe, like I do, that when one in three Native American women will be raped in their lifetimes, that is an assault on our national conscience; it is an affront to our shared humanity; it is something that we cannot allow to continue.

So ultimately, it's not just the federal government's relationship with tribal governments that compels us to act, it's not just our obligations under treaty and under law, but it's also our values as a nation that are at stake. And that's why earlier this year, after extensive consultations with tribal leaders, Attorney General Holder announced significant reforms to increase prosecutions of crimes committed in Indian Country. He hired more Assistant U.S. Attorneys and more victim-witness specialists. And he even created a position for a National Indian Country Training Coordinator who will work with prosecutors and law enforcement officers throughout Indian Country.

And under Secretary Salazar's leadership, we're launching new community policing pilot programs. We've overhauled the recruitment process for BIA officers, resulting in a 500 percent jump in applications and the largest hiring increase in history. And we're working to deploy those officers to the field as quickly as possible.

The bill I'm signing into law today will build on these efforts, because it requires the Justice Department to disclose data on cases in Indian Country that it declines to prosecute and it gives tribes greater authority to prosecute and punish criminals themselves. It expands recruitment and retention and training for BIA and Tribal officers and gives them better access to criminal databases. It includes new provisions to prevent counterfeiting of Indian-produced crafts and new guidelines and training for domestic violence and sex crimes. And it strengthens tribal courts and police departments and enhances programs to combat drug and alcohol abuse and help at-risk youth.

So these are significant measures that will empower tribal nations and make a real difference in people's lives. Because as I said during our tribal conference, I have no interest in just paying lip service to the problems we face. I know that too often, this community has heard grand promises from Washington that turned out to be little more than empty words. And I pledged to you then that if you gave me a chance, this time it would be different. I told you I was committed to moving forward and forging a new and better future together in every aspect of our government-to-government relationship.

And slowly but surely, that is exactly what we are doing. At this moment, agencies across our government are implementing detailed plans to increase coordination and consultation with tribal governments — and I intend to hold them accountable for following through.

We've also included a permanent reauthorization of the Indian Health Care Improvement Act in the health care reform legislation we passed this spring. We're strengthening Tribal education. We're working to spur economic development throughout Indian Country. And in consultation with Indian tribes, we're now formally reviewing the United Nations Declaration on the Rights of Indigenous Peoples. And after 14 long years, we've finally settled the Cobell case and we're working with Congress to get the settlement approved as quickly as possible.

So we're moving forward, and we're making progress. And as we celebrate today, I'm reminded of a visit I made a couple of years ago to the Crow Nation out in Montana. While I was there, I was adopted into the Nation by a wonderful couple — Hartford and Mary Black Eagle

— so I'm Barack Black Eagle. (Laughter.) But I was also — I was also given a Crow name that means "One Who Helps People Throughout the Land." And it's a name that I view not as an honor that I deserve, but as a responsibility that I must work to fulfill.

And looking back, I can't help but think that only in America could a guy like me named Barack Obama — adoptive son of the Crow Nation — go on to become President. (Laughter and applause.) That was improbable when it happened two years ago — (laughter) — but it would have been inconceivable a generation or two before that. And I think the same could be said of this legislation.

And that should ultimately give us all hope. It should remind us that our union has a way of — over time — becoming more, and not less, perfect — more inclusive, more fair, more free. And that's because of people like you — leaders and public servants and everyday folks who understand that we're more than just heirs to a difficult past. Here in America, we have a chance to choose a different future, and to heed those better angels of our nature and cast our lot with something bigger than ourselves.

So it's in that spirit that I hope we define the relationship between our nations in the years ahead, and it is the goal of this legislation that I am proud to sign into law today.

Thank you very much, everybody. God bless you. God bless the United States of America. (Applause.)

Chapter 13

Remarks by the President at Bill Signing For The Claims Resolution Act

December 08, 2010

Hello, everybody. (Applause.) Thank you. Thank you very much. Everybody, please have a seat. Have a seat. Welcome, everybody. We are thrilled to have you here. And I want to start by acknowledging a few people who have worked so hard to allow us to be here today on this wonderful occasion.

Our Attorney General, Eric Holder — you can give him a round of applause. Two outstanding members of my Cabinet who couldn't have worked harder to make today happen — Secretary of the Interior Ken Salazar, and Secretary of Agriculture Tom Vilsack. (Applause.) And four outstanding leaders who made it their business to see this thing through — Senator Max Baucus, Democrat of Montana; Senator Jeff Bingaman, Democrat of New Mexico; Representative Jim Clyburn, Democrat of South Carolina; and Representative Tom Cole, Republican of Oklahoma. Please give them a big round of applause. (Applause.)

And one last person who doesn't get a lot of notice but put a huge amount of time and actually crossed the T's and dotted the I's to help this thing along — my good friend from law school — even though he now looks younger than me because I've gotten the gray hair and he hasn't — (laughter) — and what's the official title? Is it deputy or — it's associate — Associate Attorney General Tom Perrelli. (Applause.)

Obviously, despite the extraordinary leadership on the stage, this also would not have gotten done without the activists, the tribal leaders, and the outstanding members of Congress -- both Democrat and Republican -- who have come together and done so much over the years to make this a reality.

Here in America, we believe that all of us are equal and that each of us deserves the chance to pursue our own version of happiness. It's what led us to become a nation. It's at the heart of who we are as a people. And our history is defined by the struggle to fulfill this ideal — to build a more perfect union, to ensure that all of us, regardless of our race or religion, our color or our creed, are afforded the same rights as Americans, and the fair and equal treatment under the law.

I think all of us understand that we haven't always lived up to those ideals. When we've fallen short, it's been up to ordinary citizens to stand up to inequality and unfairness wherever they find it. That's how we've made progress. That's how we've moved forward. And that's why we are here today — to sign a bill into law that closes a long and unfortunate chapter in our history.

First, for many years African American farmers claimed they were discriminated against when they applied for federal farm loans — making it more difficult for them to stay in business and maintain their farms. In 1999, a process was established to settle these claims. But the settlement was implemented poorly and tens of thousands of African American families who filed paperwork after the deadline were denied their chance to make their case.

And that's why, as senator, I introduced legislation to provide these farmers the right to have their claims heard. That's why I'm proud that Democrats and Republicans have come together to lay this case to rest. And that's why I'm proud that Secretary Vilsack and everybody at the Department of Agriculture are continuing to address claims of past discrimination by other farmers throughout our country.

The second case we're addressing today has to do with the responsibilities that the government has to Native Americans. It began when Elouise Cobell — who's here today — charged the Interior Department with failing to account for tens of billions of dollars that they were supposed to collect on behalf of more than 300,000 of her fellow Native Americans.

Elouise's argument was simple: The government, as a trustee of Indian funds, should be able to account for how it handles that money. And now, after 14 years of litigation, it's finally time to address the way that Native Americans were treated by their government. It's finally time to make things right.

The bipartisan agreement finalized this month will result in payments to those affected by this case. It creates a scholarship fund to help make higher education a reality for more Native Americans. It helps put more land in the hands of tribes to manage for their members. And it also includes money to settle lawsuits over water rights, giving seven tribes in Arizona, Montana and New Mexico permanent access to secure water supplies year-round.

After years of delay, this bill will provide a small measure of justice to Native Americans whose funds were held in trust by a government charged with looking out for them. And it represents a major step forward in my administration's efforts to fulfill our responsibilities and strengthen our government-to-government relationship with the tribal nations.

In the end, the work that is represented on this stage and among these members of Congress, this isn't simply a matter of making amends. It's about reaffirming our values on which this nation was founded -- principles of fairness and equality and opportunity. It's about helping families who suffered through no fault of their own get back on their feet. It's about restoring a sense of trust between the American people and the government that plays such an important role in their lives.

As long as I have the privilege of serving as your President I will continue to do everything I can to restore that trust. And that's why I am so extraordinarily proud to sign this bill today.

I want to thank once again all those members of Congress. We got a lot of members here — the Congressional Black Caucus, who I know worked the Pigford issue tirelessly. We've got, as I said, Democrats and Republicans who were supportive of this issue for so long. This is one of those issues where you don't always get political credit, but it's just the right thing to do. And I couldn't be prouder of you.

Chapter 14

Remarks by the President at Signing of the Don't Ask, Don't Tell Repeal Act of 2010

December 22, 2010

You know, I am just overwhelmed. This is a very good day. (Applause.) And I want to thank all of you, especially the people on this stage, but each and every one of you who have been working so hard on this, members of my staff who worked so hard on this. I couldn't be prouder.

Sixty-six years ago, in the dense, snow-covered forests of Western Europe, Allied Forces were beating back a massive assault in what would become known as the Battle of the Bulge. And in the final days of fighting, a regiment in the 80th Division of Patton's Third Army came under fire. The men were traveling along a narrow trail. They were exposed and they were vulnerable. Hundreds of soldiers were cut down by the enemy.

And during the firefight, a private named Lloyd Corwin tumbled 40 feet down the deep side of a ravine. And dazed and trapped, he was as good as dead. But one soldier, a friend, turned back. And with shells landing around him, amid smoke and chaos and the screams of wounded men, this soldier, this friend, scaled down the icy slope, risking his own life to bring Private Corwin to safer ground.

For the rest of his years, Lloyd credited this soldier, this friend, named Andy Lee, with saving his life, knowing he would never have made it out alone. It was a full four decades after the war, when the two friends reunited in their golden years, that Lloyd learned that the man who saved his life, his friend Andy, was gay. He had no idea. And he didn't much care. Lloyd knew what mattered. He knew what had kept him alive; what made it possible for him to come home and start a family and live the rest of his life. It was his friend.

And Lloyd's son is with us today. And he knew that valor and sacrifice are no more limited by sexual orientation than they are by race or by gender or by religion or by creed; that what made it possible for him to survive the battlefields of Europe is the reason that we are here today. (Applause.) That's the reason we are here today. (Applause.)

So this morning, I am proud to sign a law that will bring an end to "Don't Ask, Don't Tell." (Applause.) It is a law — this law I'm about to sign will strengthen our national security and uphold the ideals that our fighting men and women risk their lives to defend.

No longer will our country be denied the service of thousands of patriotic Americans who were forced to leave the military -- regardless of their skills, no matter their bravery or their zeal, no matter their years of exemplary performance -- because they happen to be gay. No longer will tens of thousands of Americans in uniform be asked to live a lie, or look over their shoulder, in order to serve the country that they love. (Applause.)

As Admiral Mike Mullen has said, "Our people sacrifice a lot for their country, including their lives. None of them should have to sacrifice their integrity as well." (Applause.)

That's why I believe this is the right thing to do for our military. That's why I believe it is the right thing to do, period.

Now, many fought long and hard to reach this day. I want to thank the Democrats and Republicans who put conviction ahead of politics to get this done together. (Applause. I want to recognize Nancy Pelosi — (applause) — Steny Hoyer — (applause) — and Harry Reid. (Applause.)

Today we're marking an historic milestone, but also the culmination of two of the most productive years in the history of Congress, in no small part because of their leadership. And so we are very grateful to them. (Applause.)

I want to thank Joe Lieberman — (applause) — and Susan Collins. (Applause.) And I think Carl Levin is still working — (laughter) — but I want to add Carl Levin. (Applause.) They held their shoulders to the wheel in the Senate. I am so proud of Susan Davis, who's on the stage. (Applause.) And a guy you might know — Barney Frank. (Applause.) They kept up the fight in the House. And I've got to acknowledge Patrick Murphy, a veteran himself, who helped lead the way in Congress. (Applause.)

I also want to commend our military leadership. Ending "Don't Ask, Don't Tell" was a topic in my first meeting with Secretary Gates, Admiral Mullen, and the Joint Chiefs. (Applause.) We talked about how to end this policy. We talked about how success in both passing and implementing this change depended on working closely with the Pentagon. And that's what we did.

And two years later, I'm confident that history will remember well the courage and the vision of Secretary Gates — (applause) — of Admiral Mike Mullen, who spoke from the heart and said what he believed was right — (applause) — of General James Cartwright, the Vice Chairman of the Joint Chiefs; and Deputy Secretary William Lynn, who is here. (Applause.) Also, the authors of the Pentagon's review, Jeh Johnson and General Carter Ham, who did outstanding and meticulous work — (applause) — and all those who laid the groundwork for this transition.

And finally, I want to express my gratitude to the men and women in this room who have worn the uniform of the United States Armed Services. (Applause.) I want to thank all the patriots who are here today, all of them who were forced to hang up their uniforms as a result of "Don't Ask, Don't Tell" — but who never stopped fighting for this country, and who rallied and who marched and fought for change. I want to thank everyone here who stood with them in that fight.

Because of these efforts, in the coming days we will begin the process laid out by this law. Now, the old policy remains in effect until Secretary Gates, Admiral Mullen and I certify the military's readiness to implement the repeal. And it's especially important for service members to remember that. But I have spoken to every one of the service chiefs and they are all committed to implementing this change swiftly and efficiently. We are not going to be dragging our feet to get this done. (Applause.)

Now, with any change, there's some apprehension. That's natural. But as Commander-in-Chief, I am certain that we can effect this transition in a way that only strengthens our military readiness; that people will look back on this moment and wonder why it was ever a source of controversy in the first place.

I have every confidence in the professionalism and patriotism of our service members. Just as they have adapted and grown stronger with each of the other changes, I know they will do so again. I know that Secretary Gates, Admiral Mullen, as well as the vast majority of service members themselves, share this view. And they share it based on their own experiences, including the experience of serving with dedicated, duty-bound service members who were also gay.

As one special operations warfighter said during the Pentagon's review — this was one of my favorites — it echoes the experience of Lloyd Corwin decades earlier: "We have a gay guy in the unit. He's big, he's mean, he kills lots of bad guys." (Laughter.) "No one cared that he was gay." (Laughter.) And I think that sums up perfectly the situation. (Applause.)

Finally, I want to speak directly to the gay men and women currently serving in our military. For a long time your service has demanded a particular kind of sacrifice. You've been asked to carry the added burden of secrecy and isolation. And all the while, you've put your lives on the line for the freedoms and privileges of citizenship that are not fully granted to you.

You're not the first to have carried this burden, for while today marks the end of a particular struggle that has lasted almost two decades, this is a moment more than two centuries in the making.

There will never be a full accounting of the heroism demonstrated by gay Americans in service to this country; their service has been obscured in history. It's been lost to prejudices that have waned in our own lifetimes. But at every turn, every crossroads in our past, we know gay Americans fought just as hard, gave just as much to protect this nation and the ideals for which it stands.

There can be little doubt there were gay soldiers who fought for American independence, who consecrated the ground at Gettysburg, who manned the trenches along the Western Front, who stormed the beaches of Iwo Jima. Their names are etched into the walls of our memorials. Their headstones dot the grounds at Arlington.

And so, as the first generation to serve openly in our Armed Forces, you will stand for all those who came before you, and you will serve as role models to all who come after. And I know that you will fulfill this responsibility with integrity and honor, just as you have every other mission with which you've been charged.

And you need to look no further than the servicemen and women in this room — distinguished officers like former Navy Commander Zoe Dunning. (Applause.) Marines like Eric Alva, one of the first Americans to be injured in Iraq. (Applause.) Leaders like Captain Jonathan Hopkins, who led a platoon into northern Iraq during the initial invasion, quelling an ethnic riot, earning a Bronze Star with valor. (Applause.) He was discharged, only to receive emails and letters from his soldiers saying they had known he was gay all along — (laughter) — and thought that he was the best commander they ever had. (Applause.)

There are a lot of stories like these — stories that only underscore the importance of enlisting the service of all who are willing to fight for this country. That's why I hope those soldiers, sailors, airmen, Marines and Coast Guardsmen who have been discharged under this discriminatory policy will seek to reenlist once the repeal is implemented. (Applause.)

That is why I say to all Americans, gay or straight, who want nothing more than to defend this country in uniform: Your country needs you, your country wants you, and we will be honored to welcome you into the ranks of the finest military the world has ever known. (Applause.)

Some of you remembered I visited Afghanistan just a few weeks ago. And while I was walking along the rope line — it was a big crowd, about 3,000 — a young woman in uniform was shaking my hand and other people were grabbing and taking pictures. And she pulled me into a hug and she whispered in my ear, "Get 'Don't Ask, Don't Tell' done." (Laughter and applause.) And I said to her, "I promise you I will." (Applause.)

For we are not a nation that says, "don't ask, don't tell." We are a nation that says, "Out of many, we are one." (Applause.) We are a nation that welcomes the service of every patriot. We are a nation that believes that all men and women are created equal. (Applause.) Those are the ideals that generations have fought for. Those are the ideals that we uphold today. And now, it is my honor to sign this bill into law. (Applause.)